The Light of God
Shines as You

The Light of God Shines as You

Betsy Hamric

THE LIGHT OF GOD SHINES AS YOU
by Betsy Hamric

FIRST EDITION 2019

ISBN 978-1-7329693-0-8

Published by Talent Books

Book layout by Palomar Print Design
Cover design by Paul Gorman

All references to the Miracle Self and all Miracle Self quotes are used with permission.

This book is dedicated to Paul F. Gorman whose life work, called the Miracle Self, revealed the mystical consciousness for me in both his work and that of Joel S. Goldsmith. I am forever grateful for this gift of the spirit. With loving gratitude I thank Paul and all who have sought God and found God and have devotedly shared the way with those whose hearts are searching for the same.

Edited by F.P.

Thank you for your loving support and collaboration
in bringing this work into actuality.

The life was in him (God), and the life (God) is the light of men. And the same light shines in darkness, and the darkness does not overcome it.

Again Jesus spoke to them, saying, I am the light of the world; he who follows me shall not walk in darkness, but he shall find for himself the light of life.

While you have the light, believe in the light, so that you may become the sons of the light.

For God, who said, Let light shine out of darkness, has shone in our hearts so that we may be enlightened with the knowledge of the glory of God in the person of Christ.

And there shall be no night there; and they shall neither need a candle nor the light of the sun; for the Lord God shines on them, and they shall reign for ever and ever.

You are a chosen people, ministers to the kingdom, a holy people, a congregation redeemed to proclaim the glories of him who has called you out of darkness to his marvelous light; You, who in the past, were not considered a people, but who are now the people of God, who had not obtained mercy, but who now have mercy poured upon you.

Arise, shine; for your light is come, and the glory of the Lord shall rise upon you. Behold, darkness will cover the earth, and thick darkness the nations; but the Lord shall shine upon you, and his glory shall be seen upon you. And the Gentiles shall come to your light, and kings to the brightness of your rising. Lift up your eyes round about and see; they all gather themselves together, they come to you ...*

---

*   John 1:4-5; John 8:12; John 12:36; 2 Corinthians 4:6; Revelation 22:5; 1 Peter 2:9-10; Isaiah 60:1-4; Holy Bible From Ancient Eastern Manuscripts by George M. Lamsa

Words of Wisdom From Joel S. Goldsmith

"The knowledge of God reveals the infinite nature of individual man. Since 'I and my Father are one'*... 'He that seeth me seeth him that sent me.'** That is how sacred the individual is. He is the showing forth of God; he is that place in consciousness where God shines through.

"... as a child of God you embody all of the power of the Godhead. You are the outlet for that spiritual power ... Spiritual power reveals 'God is in the midst of you.' Spiritual power reveals harmony, completeness, wholeness, justice, equity ...

SPIRITUAL POWER REVEALS.
Remember that.

"In this same way the prayer, meditation, or treatment of a metaphysical practitioner does not destroy disease, poverty, accident, lack, or limitation. It reveals the illusory nature of these, and in doing so it reveals the omnipresence of God.

"Understand the nature of spiritual prayer: Its function or purpose is to reveal God's grace right where the illusion, the discord, claims to be.

" ... 'Father, reveal thy grace, thy peace, thy kingdom. Thy grace is my sufficiency in all things .... Just thy grace reveals abundance....' Watch that your heart and Soul is longing only to become aware of the presence of God, the grace of God, the kingdom of God, the peace of God.'"***

*   John 10:30
**   John 12:45
***   Joel S. Goldsmith, *Consciousness Transformed*, "The Nature of Spiritual Prayer"

CONTENTS

Coming Home to the Light
Part I

CONTENTS

CONTENTS

The Vastness of the Light
Part II

CONTENTS

CONTENTS

The Light of God Shines as You Part III

CONTENTS

Coming Home to the Light
Part I

Alone in the Darkness

In the darkness
With eyes closed in meditation
It could seem
A blank cold world is before me
A scary nothingness
In which I am alone
But I am willing to be still
To grow and expand

In that within-ness
I see there is nothing scary
As a vastness
Fills my consciousness
With a sweet presence
In that seeming darkness

What is this presence
I am not sure I know
But one thing I do know
Is that I feel comfort and love

I return
To this place
Of comfort and love
Finding new treasures
Of fulfillment freely bestowed
A growing sense of something
Which loves me very much

I return day after day
And night after night
I dare not ask for a treasure
Of this darkness
I somehow know
In this presence
I have no need of asking

In some way
Unknown to me
I do know
I already have everything
Even though it is not yet
Visible to me

For now I will be content
With this darkness
With the treasures
That have been bestowed
Knowing that in this contentedness
More seems to come forth

As I cannot ask
I also cannot expect
So I have discovered
The joy
Of receiving

This joy
Of receiving melts
Into a great humility and oneness

I stop
No thought
And bask
In the beauty of being-ness
Alone in the darkness

Was I Ever Really Alone in the Darkness?

No, but I thought I was. Even the words in "Alone in the Darkness" are telling of the Light. Did you catch the sense of knowing and having, the Light Itself, the very presence of God that weaves in and out throughout the darkness here? This knowing and having are inherent in each of us although it may be covered over with many thoughts and beliefs for now.

We are the very Light of knowing and having we are looking for or don't think we have. We are the Light without doing a thing. Well, one thing. Just accept it. Just say to yourself "Yes! Yes!" instead of "no" to see it. I cannot tell you of all the many windows of heaven that will open up for you if you will catch yourself thinking or saying "no" to this or that or to what you see your neighbor or a stranger doing or saying.

Let them and your self alone, and more than that, bless all as the god being they are and you are, and all of heaven will open up with blessings all over the place. Enjoy saying "Yes!" to everything you see this way, and you will begin to smile … a lot! The world will begin to look like you have always wanted it to be.

The "no" to what we see is our own limiting thought blocking the Light, the unlimited possibilities right before our eyes. Yes, this is all that is blocking our vision, the Light we are and all are; and here, right where we are now, is the full joy of life. When we find it for ourselves, we find it for others, too, and we start seeing it everywhere. Here, right where you are, is the joy and Light of life.

First Light of Dawn

First Light of dawn
Living love
Shining forth
Eternally
As the pure soul
Of the servant
Of the Holy One
One life
One love
One immaculate
Creation and vision

In that grace
I stand
In that grace
I behold
In that grace
I know
As I am known

Here
In this grace
Is the eternal
Peace and perfection
Of man
Satisfied
In His
Likeness

In this Light of lights
The new world appears
World beyond worlds
Life beyond lives
Love beyond loves
Truth beyond truths
Unceasing joy beyond duality

I stand
In the first Light
Of dawn
I am
That Light
Eternally One
And all

Now
Touch this gently
My child
As One
Not being
Of the earth earthy

For thou art
In and of
The Holy One
Not of man
Whose breath
Is in his nostrils

Hear
My Word
That you remain
In Me
My servant
Whom I have
Loved
From the beginning

Be thou
Perfect
In Me
Continue
In the way

I Am with thee
My child of spirit
Rejoice
I say to thee
Always rejoice

First Light of dawn
Living love
Truth infinite
The miracle
Of endless oneness
Shines brightly as all that is
As you

My Dear Father Light

My Dear Father Light
Shine in me
As Me
Through me
Out to the world

May I ever
More consistently
Hear the Voice
That says
Sit in the silence
With Me

May I ever
More consistently
See the truth
Everywhere
It is not really
So difficult
As I thought
All these years

Let me entertain
No doubts
Let me not get caught
In material
Circumstances
Forget
The One
I am

Thank you
For bringing me
To the Light
Shining
As
The Miracle Self

All by
Your grace
The new day
Is
The horizon
Is fading away

All glory
To Thee
In Thee
Of Thee

Highway Robbery

Having eyes
See ye not
Having material eyes
You do not see

Having My Presence
As your focal point
Of awareness
You see truly
The beauty
The goodness
The truth
Of all that is

My Kingdom
My Way
My Being
Everywhere

You know
Not
Of your own self

Is it not
Highway robbery
To be a window
For the world
Witnessing oneness
For all
As we drop
This world

It Is I

It is I
God is
First and always
God

Never forget this
It is I
My universe
All it contains
Is mine alone

I think
It not strange
To recognize
Everyone
In truth
As the
Christ

This is
The salvation
To a human sense
Of the world

I bypass
All human belief
To walk
In the truth
As God is
For God Itself
It is I

The Call of God Is Heard

Through our hearts
Our eyes enjoy
The gentle shine
Of the morning sun
Greetings
Of the gracious mother
Of the day

Seeing the playfulness
Of the animals
As flowers absorb
The morning's
Bright blessings
The dancing sea
Leaps for pure joy
All
The beauty and joy
Of God's heaven

It takes a heart
Resting in the love
Of the infinite One
To see heaven on earth
There
The true order
Known
By the soul
Dwelling
In the eternal spirit
Of love
That is God

The beautiful scenes
Are nothing
Compared to the gentle breath
Of spirit
An ever increasing
Life
Out of the
Love
That is God

The
Free
Immortal spirit
Of God
Brings forth
The exalted thought
An invaluable
Beautiful work

The call
Of
God
Is
Heard

O Holy One

O Holy One
Spirit
Of the living God

In the heart
Of the soul
The flame
Of love
Grows bright
Bestowing the wisdom
To know
The presence
Of God

The
Light
Shines

There is
No darkness

O Holy One

Acceptance

I heard
This morning
After several attempts
To be silent
I must fully accept
The Miracle Self
I must fully accept
The Miracle Self
I am

My Kingdom
Wholly I
Holy I
Wholly
Being the truth
And Holy
Being the spirit

I saw
I was looking back
To decades
Of previous
Metaphysical teachings
Looking
For the truth and spirit
Of being
That I
From the human perspective
Had seemed to have lost

No

Here
Now
Is the Kingdom
My Kingdom
I
Of God
God
Through God
God
For God
God
The Miracle Self

Most gratefully
Full deep acceptance
Consciously known and felt
Acceptance accepted

Dear Friends,

This has been my ongoing challenge and battle within myself for about the last two years, to accept that which, for me, is obviously the Word of God, is obviously the truth Jesus taught, is obviously good, but in a human world, personal sense (belief or hypnotism) would have me say "no, no" to the Miracle Self instead of "Yes! Yes!" It's really that simple, but I had to get real about that accepting and insist on it very strongly, for personal sense resists mightily in giving up itself. It does become easier, a little more peace here and a little more love there, and we see it!

In the Beginning with God

I am the Light

The Light is all there is
That is it
Christ
Consciousness

When one knows the Light
One knows I am the Light

That is when
The inner and the outer
Are the same
The same
That was and is
In the beginning with God
The finished Kingdom*

A Meditation

I am
Universal being
There is
None other

I am always
Face to Face
With God
As universal being

There is no other
Life or law
Either within or without
Within here or out there
Neither of which exists
Because the seamless
Oneness of God
Is all there is

The work
Of hypnotism
A person
With a personal sense
Of history and world
About him or her
Is purely fictitious

Through its interpretation
Only mortal scenes
Held in mind are out pictured

It makes it seem
As if
A personal world literally is
A personal self literally is
Full of that
Which it is not
Inescapable and capricious laws
Of good and bad

There is no beginning
Nor end to God
Neither lack
Limitation
Nor disease
Of any kind

We are
That same
One
Without beginning or end
Without any limitation

As it says
In the gospel of John
The same
Was in the beginning with God

The same as God already was
Was and is not
Different from God
God being
Universal and eternal

I am
Is
The same
As God

From this infinity
Of God being
Could there possibly be
Any finite being
As we name
Past
Present
Future
Time and space

No
These are obsolete
All hypnotism
Personal belief
And personal sense
Misinterpretation

We are I am
Infinite universal being

There is
None
Other

I am always
Face to Face
With God

For My Children

Pour forth from the fountain
That seems to flow from without

Seek not your own to benefit
But all of God's own to receive

Know ye not the knowledge of man
Whose breath is in his nostrils

But the wisdom of that which
Can never be written or spoken

Ah yes!
The spirit of God
Is surely in this place

There is nothing to harm or hurt
My Child in all My Kingdom

For I Am come and I am redeemed
I am life and I am love

I Am You and I Am Me
By My everlasting grace

A Glimpse

An opening in the middle of the night communicates "completeness" in feeling and and word. There is a realization of this, and then the words came: This is your teacher," and I understood.

A couple days later in the grocery store

A young man approaches and recognizes me as a "knower." (I look it up in my books and, after reading, I do not call myself a "knower.") He said he survived a train running over him fifteen years ago and since then just knows things. I see his eyes and face are pure and clear.

He says it is true, what is written, that the world will suffer a great devastation, and without a pause I continued as only one voice speaking, "and those who understand will not be touched." His eyes opened wider a bit, were brighter. There was a soft, quiet, subtle sense of peace. He thanked me and left.

The words I said came through me, not from me. I should have thanked him, for what came through me was surely in response to his spoken words, his consciousness.

The Lamb of God,
Part 1

I am the lamb of God
The meek one
Worthy of eternal life
Of being the temple
Of the living God
I am that temple

We have not truly known
This body
That we have and are

Does its literal ability
To heal
As shown to us daily
Even continually
In this actual
Eternal life
That we are and see
That we mistakenly think
Is a physical body and world
Not tell us of its
Eternal sacred being

It is
The temple of God
Here
Now
Evident
The finished Kingdom
The temple
Not made with hands

Can this body really be matter
Does that even make sense

Worthy is the lamb
The meek one
Conscious
Only of God as all
While seeing an infinity
Of forms and experiences
All being
The Light of God
The Consciousness
God
Being all this lamb
Of God
Is aware of
As forms and experiences
Are seen and known
For what they truly are

The Lamb of God,
Part 2

This is the true Light
The true Light
Is God
That lights every man

The true Light
Is the true image

To see the true image
The true son of God
The Christ
The meek one
Here and now
Is to know
Each of us know
We as the lamb of God
Are the true Light of God
The Christ

Not material or physical
Nor of time and space
Cause or effect

The true Light
The lamb
The Light of God
Shining as all

We are Consciousness
The Light
Of being
The truth
Being the Light

The Light of truth
Shines
As the pure and literal
Consciousness
Of God
As the
Lamb of God
One and all

That Light reveals
Perfect harmony
Perfect being
Of all that is
Unconditional and eternal

Everywhere
The Light of the lamb
Is present
God being is
The only presence
The only image

The Light
The truth
Is the image

The lamb is literally
In all truth
The Light
Of the world
The Light of God

That is the
Seamless robe
That ever remains
Whole and beautiful

This was and is now
The life
Of Christ Jesus
Our Wayshower
Our same I am
The lamb

God Infallible

Would any of us be here in class after class if we had already found God as infallibility?

No human being has it, although many like to believe they have earned it or created it in a human material way of life. They have to continue to work chasing the good life to try to keep what they think is the infallible, but eventually all, at least the ones I know, run into fallibility.

It's almost guaranteed . . . except for the very few who seem to have something most are not aware of. Now we know.

The first class opened up that secret of life: God, the infallible all. How many of us, together in Consciousness, are able to open our hearts fully to accept this most precious gift from God to god, but only the One? Only as one can I, god, now see and know the all, all people, things, places, as God infallible knowing Itself.

I do nothing; I am nothing without God. God is Consciousness is my mind, and that is being, the doing and the form. I do nothing; I am nothing without God.

What a beautiful release I felt in class not to be responsible for everything!

The real beauty of all this is that it is all inclusive. It makes no divisions, no inharmony or separation, no pain in any way or form, the treasure of the infallible life, God being.

This treasure is for our entire world, and that is our greatest pleasure, to give as it has been given to us. I have known no greater one than Christ Jesus who showed us the way, the truth, and the spirit in his three years of sharing God's Word as the truth of being made visible, always the present truth, if we have eyes to see.*

---

*   Inspired notes from the class INFALLIBLE HEALING given by Paul F. Gorman

Give Your Eyes to God

Give your eyes to God
For this is loving God
With all your heart
All your soul
All your mind
And all your strength

You are
This love
As you give
Your eyes to God

~

Rest now
Feel this love
The words are nothing

~

This is loving your neighbor
As yourself
Do you feel it

Is not this the love
The life
The Light
Of the world
For this is seeing
Everyone and everything
As God

Let the shepherd
Your pure soul Consciousness
Bring you back
Into the fold
To safety
To perfection
To harmony
To the purity
You are
And all is
As the One

Arise now
Turn not
Your eyes
Away from God
For you but reject
The fullness
Of your own life

Choose ye this day
To come
To this love and Light

Come home
Again and again
To this love Light shining
For there
Is a beautiful returning
Of all God is
To you
For you
As you feel
This love Light
Flowing out
And returning
Morning to night
Night to morning

I have found my work
My offering
For the world
My eyes
My all
Are full
Of this love Light
For the world

Bow down
To this love Light
Of all that is
You and your
Mother
Father
Sister
Brother
Friend

Bow down
To this sight
Pure and good

The Light Itself
Will raise you up
Show you the way
But you must bow down
To the Light
To see the way

You must
Give your eyes
Give yourself
To the Light
You must be nothing
In Its presence

Be not content
In your own way
In your own sight
This is the truth
You never will be satisfied
With your own self
Your own vision

Your sight is devoid
Of the way
The truth
Light
The Life Itself

Let us leave
The misgiven self
Behind
The true One
Would joyfully have it so
Know Its truth
Know Itself as the Light of God

Your Light
Must shine for all
For the Light
Is all

Leave not anyone
Behind
Or you have left
God behind
The way and the Light
Behind

When you bring the One
You bring the all
Without all
You are nothing
You have nothing
All out there and in here
Is the One you are
God is all
The One

You are that same
You are all and the One
Everyone is all and the One

This is not hard to be
To do
You already understand
You already know
You already are

Only self
Will get in the way
A little
But put it aside
And carry on
Put thought and judgment
Aside
To let God
Be your eyes

Your heart
Feels it right now
If you will let it
So do the little practice
To see

Give your eyes
To God
Be not blind
Anymore

Your eyes
Are the
Light
Of God
The Light
Of the world

It is up to you
To release them
To God
So that heaven
Is seen and experienced

This is the highest
Calling
On earth
The highest purpose
The greatest blessing for all

Release yourself
Release your eyes to God
Quietly with great joy
Follow the Master

Oh! Feel that quiet depth
Of Light and love
Feel it ever deepening
As it does
Misgivings
Are melting away
Into their native nothingness

You know
The Light
Of God
The love
Of God
For
It
Is
You

This is for you
To simply accept
Your doing is only
For you to accept
Allow it to be
That's all

Yes
You know

You know
The end of struggle
Is in this accepting
This being
Of the love
The Light of God
Your native home
You never really left

Yes
Give your eyes
Your body
To God
They are his eyes
His body
His Light shining
As all you are
That he first gave
You

Not as if you are separate from Him
There is only the One

In all of heaven
And heaven on earth
There is no self
But the One
Shining as the infinite
Light
Love
Truth
You are
For you have given
Your eyes To God

Holy "Acts of Awareness"

Focus on a point in thin air not attached to anything physical. This tiny point of nothingness is your open door to all that is, the truth and the spirit, the beauty, the bounty and perfection of all that is, the very way, the truth, and the life.

This focal point is awareness itself, the way, the truth, the life. Hear it: your life, my life, all life, the living truth. The act of awareness is your very life now, the source of the visible life here and now. The act of awareness is literally your body, all life, all being.

My I am, your I am, everyone's I am is that infinite point of awareness. Now see there is only the One, one being, one life, infinite and eternal oneness: spirit and truth, but only the One.

An act of awareness, an act of oneness, is like giving all your senses to God. All the senses and all of the world and universe are only for revealing God to us, all that we are as all that life is. I am that I Am. You are that I Am that life is. I am that I Am. You are that I Am.

The act of awareness is the greatest act of all, full and overflowing with God's love, for it holds the key, even the free offering of God Itself to all for healing, for wholeness, as the ever-present reality the whole world is seeking. Do not miss this! The act of being the awareness of God is the healing agent in our world.*

---

* This flowed through the silence after listening to the class "Infinity of Being," ACTS OF AWARENESS, given by Paul F. Gorman.

The Way

The way
Is always yes!
Yes!
As Jesus said
Agree quickly
With thine adversary
While you are
With him*

There is only
An adversary
When we are taking
An opposite
Point of view

There is none such
In the
Kingdom of God
The heaven of God
This earth

---

*   Matthew 5:25

Home

I felt
An inner Something
Begin to take over
To make Itself known
Much more than before

"Be patient My child"
I heard
"For the seed hidden within
Must first be nourished
Grow within
Silently
Unknown for a while
To the outer

"Be aware
That you want nothing
From the outer
The inner is the outer
The root must first
Become sturdy
Before the outer
Blossoms
Into its
Full beauty and bounty

"You know now
You are mine
You are home
You have returned unto Me"

The Vastness of the Light
Part II

This Is Heaven

I Am
I have
One
There is none else

The omnipresent experience
Awareness unexplained
Abounding visibility
Now

This is heaven
Your heart confirms this
Now

It is done
I am
I Am

In the waters of truth
You are baptized
The ever new One
Risen*

Amen

---

*   Inspired notes from a class by Paul F. Gorman: *I Am, I Have* (weekend), "Treasure In Heaven"

The Silent I Am

I close my eyes
I have let
Too much
Of the world
Swallow me up
So I close my eyes

The Finished kingdom
Comes to mind

I am
Touched and uplifted
By a quiet vibration
Of
Beauty
Peace
Love

I feel
An infinite expansion
With no pictures formed
An all inclusive
Harmony
A perfection
Of
Being

I am satisfied
More than satisfied

All is well
All is well with my soul

I am
Love
Silence
Peace

I accept
I say
"Yes"
Most deeply
Grateful

Before I would have said
"No"
And not have known
The
Beauty
Peace
Love
Of the
Silent I Am

You Are Mine

"You are mine"
Says the Lord
I Am
All there is
To
You

I Am
The bread
The wine
The water

I Am
Your substance
Your body
Your mind

There is nothing
Else
To
You

Hear it
I Am I have
I Am literally I have

You
Dear ones

The infinity
You continually see
Is the Light
Of your own eyes
All of it
Yours
In a new way
You have
Never seen before

It is not yours
To appropriate
But it all comes forth
From you
It is you
You
The infinite Light

Therefore be alive
To the infinite
One
Alone

That your eyes
Shine clearly
For your
Mother
Father
Sister
Brother
Friend
The world
All
As only
The infinite
One

Let not your eyes
Wander out
To forms
Of matter
And your mind
Make them
Your life

You
I am
Are the perfect
I Am
Infinitely
Abounding and blessed

Materiality
Has no reality
In life
But will make it
Seem to be
If you accept it

Are not these words
Filled with
The love story
Of
You

Arise
In that love
Everlasting

Let that love
Live you

You will see
What I see

All
In the world
Of I Am
Joins
In perfect harmony
Fulfillment

Greater love has no man
"You are mine"
Says
The Lord

The New Life

The new life
Peace and calm
Beyond measure
A vast new expanse
Of being
Known and felt
In wordless emptiness

I arise in a vastness
Of nothing wrong
Under the sun

As all was
Before the sun
Before material life
The sun
Son
Life
The Christ
God of God
All is
After the sun
The Son
Shows up
In material being-ness

The same
One
Before the sun
As after the sun
The finished Kingdom
Silence

~

These phrases
Of thanksgiving and praise
Come to mind
I sang in church
From the time
I was a child
That I have always
Loved and remembered
With a beautiful new meaning
For me now

Praise God
From whom
All blessings flow
Praise Him
All creatures here below
Praise Him
Above ye heavenly host
Praise Father
Son
And Holy Ghost

The Lord
Is in his Holy Temple
Let all the earth
Keep silence before Him
Keep silence
Keep silence
Keep silence
Before Him

~

After this
I just thought
I would go back
To sleep
As usual
The same self
As before
But it was not
To be

I was drawn deeply
Into meditation
There appeared
And I felt
A vastness
That continued
Into the day

In that vastness
Something took over
I do not know
What happened
But I felt it
Take over
In the vastness

Something new
Made its appearance
In my mind
At least that is what I felt

The significant thing is
In that vastness
Truth and belief
Are easily distinguished
Seen
And there is nothing wrong
Under the sun
Kept showing itself
To me

As there was still no sleep
To be had
I addressed
The "laundry list"
Gently and simply
So as not
To make it real
Seeing beyond or through
To evidencing
The truth of reality
Basking
In the beauty
And freedom
Of this new dimension
Letting it be
Consciously
As the unspeakable peace
Continued

In Silence

God is
The Word
I am
The Word
You are
The Word

What comes through
Is
The Word
Not words
The
One

In the beginning
Includes everything
Before and after
There is nothing different
Under the sun
Only
The One
The
Word

A Meditation

The One
There is only
The Son
That is Me
That is You
The One
My Son

That is why
Everything
Everything
Is
Even now
Always
Perfectly fulfilled
Satisfied

The Same Light Seeing the World
Is Being the World

I am the Light
I am the One
I am the all
Of God
The pure soul

Personal sense
Is nonexistent
In the Light
Of the soul
Of God

The scales
Of human thought
Fall away
From the eyes
Revealing
The infinite fullness
Of the Light
I am and all is
All being
Good
Beautiful
True

Listen to the silence
Bathe in the silent Light
It will speak
The truth of the world
To you
Into visible existence

We come forth
From the breath
The inspiration
Of the One
From inner to outer
Meaning
From inspiration
To visibility
One and the same
Instant and eternal reality
Having nothing to do
With matter

"Every Breath of Me"

"Every breath of Me"
Is
To inspire
Is
To make visible
The essence
Of life itself
The expiration
The release
As the flow
Inspiration and expiration
Not two
Separate things
But one
The
One
Made evident*

---

*   These are the words of Paul F. Gorman, whose every breath is
to make evident to all the truth they are and all is. His message and
consciousness are throughout these writings, including his words: "Every
breath of Me."

Note to a Dear Friend

As I was in meditation
Just now
Having read your message
Many times
"Trust the reality
Of your Consciousness
As being
The very presence and visibility
Of God
Good"
I realized
I am that I Am
Consciousness
God
As the only
The realization itself
The Truth Itself
The Light

As I considered
God
Consciousness
To be
The presence and visibility
The Light
The Truth Itself
I was shown
The seed and mature tree
One
Fully complete and infinite

When I know
Am aware of
God Consciousness
And the fullness thereof
I need
Nothing else
I need
Do nothing else
I need
No idea
About this or that
No words
To think about

When I know
Consciousness is I
The one I
That is all
For Consciousness
God
Is all and is one
Then again
There is
Nothing
To do
To think
To know

This is so simple
So freeing
Truly a blessing

Thank you!
Thank you!

Second Note to a Dear Friend

I see ever clearer
Consciousness
As the pure ground
The atmosphere
Of being
Of all
Pure as always
Undefiled and untouched
By anything
The infinite pure and perfect
Unchanging One
The same
One

~

As the first few verses
In the gospel of John
Keep coming to me
To know and to be
To replace "the Word"
With "Consciousness"
In these verses
Gives me more clarity
Realization
This morning

In the beginning
Was Consciousness
And Consciousness
Was with God
And Consciousness
Was God
Consciousness is God

The same I
Consciousness
Was in the beginning
With God
All is Consciousness
Because all is God
God is all

It came to me
A long time ago
That which
I am with
I am
But my thought
Could not
Take it any deeper
At the time

Now I see
As I am with
Pure
Consciousness
As the Word
The Voice Itself
Then I am that I Am
And this makes
True and logical
The next verse

The same
Was in the beginning
With God
The seed and the tree
Fully finished
And all the host
Of them
You and me
That same I am I Am
Complete and whole
Not growing and becoming
Already the finished kingdom[*]

I am
That same
I Am

---

*   Genesis 2:1-5

You are
That same
I Am

Yes
I saw it before
But I did not understand

Now there is
Not only
Trust
There is
Understanding
Realization
Of the truth
Oneness

Thank You Meditation

In the stillness
The silence
Pure and simple
I heard the words
"I am"

I heard them again
In the purity
Of oneness
Even with
A noisy lawnmower
Next door

I hear next
"I am that I Am"

Soon after
It came
Again
In the silence
"I am that I Am"

A rare airplane flew over
The peace
Of the silence
Continued
All included and blessed
By the presence
Of God

Yesterday
I would have
Denied
God's presence
By complaining
About noisy machines

Did not I
Already recognize
Somewhere
In these writings
That God
Made
All that is made

Thank You
For the friendly reminder
That You are
All in all
All of all
All for all

The Majesty and Glory of God

As I read again
My letters
To a dear friend
I see a breaking through
Material sense

This recognition
Lifted me
Into a beautiful state
Of being

Reading
The last sentence
Of the
"Thank You Meditation"
I saw
Something new
In the words
"We are the
Majesty and glory
Of God"

Having nothing to do
With a personal self
I do see and know
The truth of all

Is this not
God's infinite vision
That I am
And you are
That same
Majesty and glory
Of God

Being Face to Face
With God
I am lifted up
I draw all men
Unto Me
In oneness
Joy
Love
Peace

To see truly
Face to Face
With God
Is to be
The majesty and glory
Of God
The greatest gift
One can share
With another

Face to Face
With God
The only presence
The majesty and glory
Of God

That You May Have Light

I Am come
That you may have Light
That your Light
May be full

Bear witness
To God
There is the true Life
Itself
The Light
The evidence

You are already
Everything
That God is
All
The presence
Of God
Now

I
Consciousness
Infinity

Wake up to I
The Light
Constant fulfillment

All is
One
Infinity
Awareness I Itself
The Kingdom
Of God
The universe
Of Light
Omnipresent

We discover
The infinite Light
Of truth
As ourselves
Complete and fulfilled
All forms
The Light
Of God

The Light
Of truth
Witnesses
The infinity
Of
Itself

I am standing
On holy ground
The Light always Itself
Perfectly fulfilled
In its own infinity
Of being

I belong
To You
You
Belong
To Me
We are
Inseparable I

I am the light
Of Light
And all
That therein is

Only God
Exists
Only I
Nothing different
From Me

The kingdom is I
Awareness I
Me
My Being
I

I
Will never
Leave You
It is I
Ever with Me
I
Awareness

All
I have
Is
Yours

All
You have
Is I
Mine

Awareness is
The Light
Of God
Is Me

One visibility
The Light
The same
One
Infinity

Awareness
Is
Seeing
Light
Confirming
The infinity
Of God
I
Awareness

All
Our work
Is within

The Kingdom
Of God
Is within

We are
The body
Of truth
The Light

I Am the Light of the World

I Am
The Light
Of the
World

The material world
Is
Nothing
Of its own self
Nothing

Leave it
Alone

Do not try
To fix
The world
Of anything

The anything
Does not exist

The Light
Is
Finished
Complete
Perfect
God
All

The infinity
Of God
Being
Is
The Light

I am
The Light
Of God
You are
The Light
Of God

The Light
Is
The witness
Of God

That is all
And miracles
Are seen

The One True Being

The
One
True
Being
Is
A god
Aware
As a god
The Light
Of the world
Consciously
Evidencing
Fulfillment
Seen visibly by
Acts of awareness

Where Problems
Apear
Hypnotism
Is
Operating

Only God
Is god
Detached
From appearance
From the human mind
Of matter

Because God
Is all
The Light of God
Is all
God being
God
The visibility
Of spirit and truth
The fulfillment
Of perfect
Being
For the all
That is
One

Rest the mind
In God
And you will
See
God
The Light

Before
I was
Blind

Now
I see

I am
The Light
I am
The truth

God is all
I am
A god

I am
The Light
Of
God

I am
The activity
Of
God

I am
The Consciousness
Of
God

God
Is all there is
To a
God

God
Fills
His
Godchild
With all
He is

Nothing missing
Nothing wrong
Nothing to do

Filled with
The presence
Of God
Is
God

My Father's House

The
Multidimensional
Universe
Spirit and truth
Consciousness

The many places
We go
In
Consciousness

Are these not
The many
Rooms
In
My Father's house

Is this not
The multidimensional
Consciousness
We are
Every time
We interface
With another

Is this not
The multidimensional
Self
Sharing
With one another
Being the sharing
Itself
Of Itself
With Itself
In the
Multidimensional
Universe

All
One
In
My Fathers house*

---

*   Inspired notes from a class by Paul F. Gorman: *I Am, I Have* (weekend), "One"

The Good One

Be
An act of
Awareness
Now
I
Incorporeal
The Good
One
The Consciousness
Of God
For
All people
But only
One
Only
God
The Good
One
God
Itself
For Itself
For all*

---

*   Inspired notes from a class by Paul F. Gorman: *I Am, I Have* (weekend), "Treasure In Heaven"

The Heavenly Treasure

We have God
Not
As a human

We are
God
As I Am
I am that I Am

With God
All already is
I
Heaven
True
I

I know
Thee
Who
Thou art

I don't care
About anything
Except
God
Then all my universe
Is cared for
For God is
Wherever I am

Love
Is the
Image
Of perfection
Always
Showing up

Will you see
Will you love

Will you love God
With
One heart
With
One soul
With
One mind
With
One strength

Now we are
Loving
Our neighbor
As
Ourselves

The heavenly treasure
Known through
Awareness
Is this love
The act of God I am
One
The present reality
Everlasting
Now[*]

I

Never look
For your life
I
Out
There

Only God
Is god
Is I am

As you have
Always
Been given
Give I
Share I
With everyone
In
Consciousness
Letting
It
Flow out
Visibly
To all

The straight and narrow way
Is
I

This will show up
For you
As all
You could ever
Imagine*

---

*   Inspired notes from a class given byPaul F. Gorman: *I Am, I Have* (weekend), He That is Least Shall Be Great"

Give God to the World

Bathe
In the waters
Of truth

Be
Raised
Up

This
Is
The new day

The One
Who is great
Serves

The child
Of God
Ministers
For
The salvation
Of all

You are gods*
A god
Gives
To all
Creation

---

*   Psalm 82:6

Humble
Invisible
Quiet

Seek
Not
To attain

Walk
Not
With ambition

Quiet
Humble
Listening
"For the Design"
To witness
To the world
In silence
Invisible

Quietly
Confidently
With faith
Trust

Stay in God
As the god
Of your universe

Be the Light
The food
The supply
The good
For the world

Bring harmony
Comfort
Healing
Freedom
From the prison
Of belief

Still the storms
All the unreal
Revealing
Eternal
Truth
Love
Peace
Harmony
Made evident
As our business

Give
Always be
Giving
As
A transparent window
Of God
Still
Empty

Give God
To the world
The greatest joy
Your only purpose
And fulfillment

Serve
In every way
Possible
In spirit
In truth
In form*

---

*   Inspired notes from a class given by Paul F. Gorman: *I Am, I Have*
(weekend),"He That Is Least Shall Be Great"

The Vastness

I have always
Loved
The inner
Expansiveness
As I felt it
This morning

I recognized
That wonderful place
Of
Love
Still felt
More material
Than of spirit
Itself

As the vastness
Expanded
This treasure
I have come to love
That's it!
This vastness
Is
Love

But still it has
A feeling
Of the physical realm
For me

What
Is
Beyond
This
I asked
As I let
Love
That vastness
Expand
Into infinity
Into seeming nothingness

There it is!
The great infinity
Love
Beyond human borders
The true
Love

Expand
With love
Beyond your borders

Expand
With love
Until you know
Nothing
And you are still

~

Rest in this
Expansive love now

~

Do you feel it
Let it rise
And you with it
In that beyond

These words
Are beautiful
So full of
Love
But this
That is yet
To be written
The most
Beautiful
Of all

Come
With your
Love
With me
Now

For when I saw
This
From a class
"All is within
Simply sensed
Expansively"*
Immediately
I knew
Oneness
The infinity
Of love

No other words
No descriptions
No coincidence

Just
Oneness

---

*   From a class by Paul F. Gorman: *I Am, I Have*, "Actual Versus Believed God Experience"

Or maybe
Just maybe
All coincidence
Is
God
One
Happening
Moment by moment
For us
To know
The One
To return us
To the
One

The Light of God Shines as You
Part III

Dear Father

Dear Father
Let me hear
That I may know
That I may understand
What it is
I can be
For You
What it is
You are for all
That all may know
Be blessed

What
is
The way
The way
Of Christ
We are told
We are
In truth

How do
We see
How do
We know
What is it
That You are
That we are

"Give thanks
For
The One
To
The One"
I heard

I am told
The pure soul
Of me
Knows

Give thanks
And hear it
It will speak
To you
It will tell you
The truth
And the way of it

The access
You have found
Is the point
Of nothingness
The act
Of awareness
God's infinity
Of Itself
Being you

This is
The interface
For you and the world
Where blessings and joy
Are the true life
Lived
Here and now
The pure soul
Of you
Of all
Unmasked
Living
The life
Of all
God
Is

You
Are
The same
God
Abundant
Infinite
Eternal
Good

But how do we
See it
Live it
Be it

How do we know
Live
The One
The oneness
As and for all

How do
I see this
How do
I live this
How can
Others also

The answer
"You already have
The key"

Now think
About
The healings
The way
Of the Wayshower

What are healings
Recognize them
For what they are
Not for what
They appear to be

Now let your thought
Go beyond
And behind
What is seen

There
His Consciousness
That point
Of awareness
That
Infinite
Invisible
Point
In space
Where nothing
Appears

There
See
The infinite One
Abundant
Love and perfection
The love and perfection
You are

Jesus sees
Truth
Always looking
Beyond
Human sight

Catch yourself
Seeing matter

Refocus

Your answer is
Holy
"Acts of Awareness"*

---

*   Inspired notes from the class *Acts of Awareness* by Paul F. Gorman

Released

Ah!
Now I see
The tremendous blessing
Of having
So many burdens
The appearances
Of this world
Some still here

But I just saw
Through it all

There is no way
I can do anything
About these problems
Some of decades

Did you hear
There is no way
Even if I want to
I cannot
Absolutely cannot
Be responsible
Be of any help

Something
In me
Just now
In this realization
Cleared responsibility
Right out of me

The freedom!
Thank you!
Thank you!

The release
I cannot explain
But I would want
All reading this
To be released
In this same way
Now
Into the
Love and peace
Of God

The Love
And peace of God
Is
The perfection
Of being

Something New

I see
Something new
In the silence

The question asks
How is it
A teacher
Comes to be
A teacher

Is it not
Being attuned
In the silence
The Voice is heard

Is it not
Living the Word
Giving the Word
To the world

Is it
Not being so busy
With material life
Managing a busy human
But listening to the Voice

Hearing
Does not come
So easily or quickly
Really listening
Deeply

Too often
The Word
Is smothered
By the
Noisy
Human mind

But with the
Consciousness
Of a teacher
One
Who has come
This way before
We may safely
Cross
The bridge
Of our
Humanity

That brings us
More and more
Into the
Presence
Of God

The place where
All
Are welcomed
Home
With the words
I am that I Am
Already

Each time
The words
Are heard
They sink in
A little more
Become more real
Until the day
More silence comes
And we feel
The great peace
Of those
Who have abandoned
Themselves
To God

Dear Friends,

Experiences like this do not repeat themselves or occur often for now, but as we dedicate more time and depth to the silence pushing beyond inner barriers, conditioned material sense belief, we expand into an ever increasing vastness that is our love and joy and peace within and in the world. I have noticed that the deepening within occurs along with gifts of the spirit and more giving without.

It is not easy to give up the human self, so know that your every effort and devotion, your dedication, is a much greater work and benefit than you as a personal self can ever sense. As we go within more, we have more peeks into the heavenly reality that we actually already are, and we feel it. I experience it a little here and there, although not fully yet, but I remain satisfied with God alone.

Beginning to See

In the midst of some very uncomfortable inner chaos, I did not see through some unspecified belief and belief forms painfully felt while I was editing a transcript. I stopped and rested in silence, even as it felt like total unrelenting upheaval within, but I did not turn to any human means of relief.

It felt like I was going through torture, of course the torture of my own making in some way. Ah, now I might be beginning to see! As I gently and consciously relaxed into the silence, being the true vision but not understanding humanly, I was released in a surprisingly short time.

Later that day I observed a situation at home taking an entirely different and unexpected positive direction. Also, my sister, who had a minor surgery a week earlier, was in a car wreck during this time that totaled her car, and she walked away with no injury. They said that was a miracle.

Now, I see. This is the way it works. As we remain God focused, God centered in our attention, then the world shifts before our eyes. Human material conditions give way to, are seen as, the Kingdom of God, perfectly fulfilled here and now as it always has been and forever will be.

God and God Alone

Put your fears
Aside

Go to God
For
God alone

There is
Only
One life

God
Living
You
Me
All

We do not
Go
To God
For
Anything
Of
The world

God alone
Already made
All
That
Is

It
Is
Perfect

It
Is
God
God alone

The Kingdom
Whole
Finished
Blessed and sanctified
By God

Do
What God
Would have you do
Only as a gift
To God
With abundant
Love and gratitude

Put all
Other
Thoughts
Aside
Though
They feel
Very powerful
For now

All
Is
God being
Now
If we have
Eyes
To see

Most of us
Are still
Learning
To see
The opportunity
This dear
Universe
Offers
To all
Who are willing

It is always
Only
Showing forth
God and God alone

More Meditation Please

I wondered
Why something
Felt different
Yesterday

I noticed
More open time
To meditate

Last night
The 9-12 pm
Meditation
Kept going
Lifting
Then more
Meditation
Again
For a couple hours
During what is
Usually
Sleep time

When I thought
I was to get up
This morning
For the usual
Morning routine
I was instructed
To meditate more
There the beauty and peace
Completeness and silence

My emails
Revealed
The reason
For more meditations
The reason
For more time available
For the distinctive impulse
That showed up
In the last meditation

That the kingdom of God
Be seen
Be made manifest
In all its truth
Its beauty
Its Light
For all
To know
To live
In perfect
Harmony and fulfillment

Infinity Calling

The Christ Consciousness is making Itself known today. We feel the pushing through of this Consciousness because God, Consciousness Itself, is infinite. As we still live to any extent in a limited material world, we will feel this pushing.

We may feel it as a certain dissatisfaction with where we are spiritually, but put that aside for the misleading belief it is. We all feel this push and will continue to until we know we are infinity, the same as God is. So, let it not be too troublesome, and let us get on with our work, however it shows up.

Soon we see that infinity makes itself known again as love, perfection, beauty, joy, and fulfillment. We cannot deny that we are gods, the same as God, the very infinity of love, joy, perfection, and abundance. We are this every hour, every second.

I am a god, and you are a god by the authority of God, Truth Itself, and nothing other than or less than God can make us otherwise. God is the one authority. There is no other authority than God, not even what appears as a physical universe or what our thoughts about the universe show us second by second.

A lesser authority cannot be authority. We are to take God authority, the truth, as our one and only authority as we are all gods of God. This is also "the call," God's call, the Voice, for us take up our work. At some point, everyone will hear the call, leave human ways and belief behind and find life and love abounding everywhere. God being all, the call comes to all.

Now realize, as uncomfortable as we may be at times that we are not measuring up to the Christ, our little bit is assuredly enough! Think about it: You have found the way. You and I are on the way, the way of Christ. Yes, we are toddlers at the moment, but many, many millions have not even recognized the way. Pioneers always have some tough work to clear the path for others to follow.

We can be so grateful to Christ Jesus, to Mary Baker Eddy, to Joel Goldsmith and to the many truth teachers, whether here or not, for dedicating their lives to the Christ message so that it is made available to us and to many more to come. You are very important, no matter how far along you think you are or are not.

It is the spirit of God in us that has us here, not we ourselves. I cannot do otherwise. The work of God is my work and your work and will some day be the work of all because the activity of God is you, is me, is all being. The being of God is your being and mine and all. The infinite One is the infinity of you, me, and all, boundless beauty and perfection, God, the truth of all. We will feel the push of infinity, even in every practical way, until we know we are that infinity, the same as God.

The Sanctuary

I
Live
Move
Have
My being
In the
Pristine sanctuary
Of the
Light
Consciousness
God
Where nothing enters
That defiles
Or makes a lie

This is seeing truly

The Father says
I Am
One
The only
The truth
The life
The way

To be
With God
For God
Is
The only work
There is
And everything else
Gets done

When I am
Knowing
Truth
God
I am loving
God
My neighbor

This is
The first
And second
Commandments
Fulfilled

I must
Consciously
Realize this
For the statement
To be true
Or have
Any real meaning

A Vision

Gliding
On an eagle
Arms spread out
Over its mighty wings
In the warmth
And light
Of the sun

In pure silence
By the eagle
By Christ
The Light
We are raised up

Only by Christ
Do we rise as
Conscious Light
True
Being

Dear Friends,

I am, we all are the eagle, the Christ soaring ever higher as the freedom and Light of God, that we know we are. Our God Light shines infinitely ever widening and lengthening, lighting up the whole universe. We then see our Light of Light shining as all that is. We see the complete and perfect universe of God that is our universe. Do you catch hold of the wondrous purpose at hand, our purpose to fulfill as we are that I Am?

Qualified Only By God

No matter
How far along we are
On our paths
We never
Really qualify
For anything
Based on
Ourselves

As much as
Shortcomings
Only beliefs
Try to press
I
Will not let
These images
Of nothingness
Have their way

I am is I Am
Never touched
Never affected
By images

The only way
Is God's way
To know
To see
To be

The Wordless Prayer

I listened in the silence
For an hour
Maybe more

Something blossomed
Within
Went forth
Into the world
As God's prayer
Shared with His universe
As I Am
One and all

This is you
Dear friends
I am

The many facets
Of the wordless prayer
The beauty
The love
The clarity
The atmosphere
So beyond anything
Known humanly

I would have loved
To have captured it
To share
With my spiritual family
But I would not interfere
With God
For sure

It lifted me on high
Carried me
Gently and lightly
In the true reality
Of the being
Of all

Feel this very quietly
My friends
We are right here
Together
Right now

Dear Friends,

This prayer is for all of us on this journey. It is helpful to remember, in the face of all the outer evidence not corroborating our spiritual perfection and being, that Jesus faced, almost daily in his three years of healing and teaching, the same conditions, the whole gamut of human ungodliness, disease, and limitation.

We are called to be here to do the work of our Wayshower, to know who we are and to not get caught in the net of material images. Here is the point of demarcation, of letting go the material sense as substance and life by mastering self. Mastering self shows up as the new world, heaven on earth. To do that we must follow the Master. Jesus lived and now lives as the true Self, the Christ of God.

Jesus' works were works of Consciousness, full of only the truth of God, of spirit. This has nothing to do with a human self, which is only personal sense. The misinterpretation of the true Self, as described in the Miracle Self, is all about revealing who and what we truly are, the same as Jesus' mission on earth.

We only have to be open one little bit, and when we close up over and over, keep on opening up over and over. That's the work, and we can do that much, but we won't necessarily get the feedback that we are used to with first efforts in this world.

Remember, when it seems we as personal sense are not enough, agree quickly with thine adversary, personal sense. Then smile. Let your self be released gently with love, that is, feeling God's love. Jesus did not let personal sense linger and continue to talk in his ear about how he was only human. He turned from personal sense to hear the Voice, God speaking.

We know he did not continue to listen to that interpretation, and he certainly did not let those words, and that is all they are, just words, define who and what he was and is now. Life is eternal and eternally good, no matter what seems to be.

He also did the work we are doing in staying open to God and accepting God's Word and work as we are also doing through classes, study, meditation, silence, seeing through the material sense of lack and limitation, and in other practical ways.

God's Love Pouring, Pouring

Ah!
Caught myself
Reacting

But I noticed
Almost instantly
I had let it go

And later
That I had not
Carried it
With me

Definitely
Not the norm

Too often I let it
Continue
To define
Who and what I am

Such a wonderful freedom!

It is God's love
Pouring pouring pouring pouring
Unceasing pouring
Continues

That love
The golden Light
Appears
More felt than seen
So beautiful

Oh!
To sit in the silence
Of that love
Like this for weeks

I hear
The word multitude
Within

It translates itself
As the multitude
Of God's love
Being
All of us
Everyone
Everything
Everywhere
Love

I feel
That love pouring
So much love
Pouring
Pouring
Pouring

It must be the
The Holy Presence of God

The Womb and a Note

Born in a womb
Of sublime gracious
Tenderness
The whole world
Present
In complete yielding
To the One

The womb
Of that gracious
Tender life
Of the beauty
Of silence

None otherness left
No push and pull
Of the senses

No unfulfilled dreams
Trying to manifest

In the womb
Yet being born
Of the womb
All at once

Stillness
One
Nothing left out

I hear the world
And all
Going on
Yet it seems
Not binding
Just there
A serenity
The beauty
Of being

The truth present
For the revelation
Of last night
Coming
After a communion
A yielding
And immersion
In Romans 1:20

The infinity
The boundless being-ness
The beauty
Of God witnessing
Itself to Itself
Us
In a way
The senses can receive
And that does clothe us
In this world

Dear Friends,

This note with a very different feeling followed.

We become, show up as, what we are consciously aware of, the being we are, god as God is. The world becomes, shows up as this One as we are this One. Only God is.

To do: Tenderly, patiently, lovingly yield up in our lives personal mundane issues of no importance. That is letting go of "I want things my way," as if there could be any activity other than God being all there is, including all activity! Clearly our delineating what we would want is personal sense preempting God's perfect eternal infinite activity.

The result: A core strength and unselfish autonomy is felt unfolding.

I Am with You

I Am with you
Til the end of time[*]
All my work is good
There shall no harm
Come to anyone
In all my world

In all my Kingdom
I Am here
I Am good
I Am all
I Am
You

"For behold I want it so"

---

[*] When the experience of time ends for each of us, we know and we are the infinity of God being.

The Remnant and Its Treasure

A definite new way of being is emerging, a deepening, even now as being the Light of Christ, seeing as Jesus saw, not the outward material corporeal person or thing but the infinite purity of being. A lifting up as the Light and love of the message from a class is right here with me. That Light and love automatically include my neighbor as myself, you and all.

There is a certain oneness, but not with the forms themselves although they are not separate from the Light and love. I am seeing through the human material scene to the inner infinite truth of being and have noticed that the spiritual truth is much more consistently being recognized where before the misinterpretation too easily slipped in and took lodging without being challenged.

This depth is precious and new with its recognition and spiritual vision actually being the practice. This is what I have been missing on my spiritual path for decades. The gift of spirit comes with opening up and opening up more, and accepting the pure teaching, and doing this over and over, and being willing to serve in practical ways the teaching and the teacher, who is a precious treasure to find.

Teachings, such as the Miracle Self, are drawing the remnant, spoken of in the Bible, back to the Word, the Light, the love, to God. This remnant holds a treasure for the world that must be nurtured and blossom for all.

I see, for those who commit and serve, a great opening for themselves and for all mankind, where all are taken in, wounds healed, and all are fed with the true food of life, the eternal and infinite Word. The world is now heaven, the Light, the love that is God, and all shall come to know and understand.

Secret of the Vastness

Yes
This is the vastness
Now opening up
Its secrets
To you

You were never
In
The vastness
As it felt at first

You
Are the vastness
This vastness
Incorporeal
I

Literally
The infinity
Of God
Spirit

You
Are a
Blessing
To your
Whole
Universe

Be aware
It will
Show up
Everywhere
For God made
All
That is made
Nothing
That God
Did not make
Is

Now
Be with this
Let it swallow you up
In its infinity
Of love and joy
Blessing all in and beyond
Our universe

The Shift

I quickly awaken
In this feeling of trust
I know God
Here
On earth
The Christ
God Man

There occurs
A perceptible shift
From person
Looking out
For God
To God
Looking out
Through knowing eyes
Through me
As I

No God and
Just the One
Consciously known

It is
I am
Of pure eyes
The Light
Seeing
I
Am

I Found the One

In my
Tattered dirty clothes
You invited me
To the feast
And kept
Inviting me

I accepted
And continued
To accept
To come
To eat
Of the Word
Of Life

Even in my
Tattered dirty clothes
My worldly
Misgivings
Lacks
Dependencies
You called to Me
And invited Me
To come
Again
And again

I found the
One
Whose devotion
Depth of Being
Are beyond
This world

There came
A trust
In the middle
Of the night
Where no time
Exists
Neither night
Nor day
An accountable
Sure trust
That God
The Light
Is Man

Life Is

There is nowhere to go
There is nowhere to leave

There is nothing to get
There is nothing to let go of

There is not too much
There is not too little

Life is not hard
Life is not easy

Life Is God
Life is good

The Light of God
The only Life

God Is
Life Is
Let it be!

The Light of God Shines as You

God sees and knows
As you
For you

You will never again
Be
What you think
You are

God
Seeing and knowing
Is you
Your world
Your universe
All that it contains

As you bathe
In this
Seeing and knowing
Light and love
You know
That is all
There is
The Light
Of God
Shining
As
You

Lift me up Father
In your Light
Your love
Your freedom
By thy grace
In conscious awareness
That I may know
Thy Kingdom come
Here and now
Your glory
My only reality

Amen

Made in the USA
Middletown, DE
06 November 2019